IN

An exploration of
Kingston upon Thames

by Michael Davison

Foreword by June Sampson

The Kingston upon Thames Society
in association with the *Surrey Comet*

With support from Millennium Festival Awards for All

PUBLIC ART IN A MARKET TOWN

Design and map by
TONY LEITCH

First edition © 2000
Published by the Kingston upon Thames Society
5 St Albans Road, Kingston upon Thames, Surrey, KT2 5HQ
in association with the *Surrey Comet*.

For invaluable help in preparing this booklet the author is indebted
to June Sampson and her authoritative books and *Surrey Comet*
features; to Anne McCormack, Tim Everson and Jill Lamb of the
Kingston Museum and Heritage Service; to Charles Ryder, Davina
Thackara and Fran Lloyd of the Faculty of Design, Kingston
University; to Martin Higgins and George Hunter of the borough's
Planning Department; and to Georgina Hall, Tony Anstee, Vernon
Crofts, John Duell, John Pink, Leslie Rendell and Joanna Smart.
He also wishes to thank Tony Leitch for his enthusiastic support.

British Library Cataloguing-in-Publication Data. A catalogue record
for this publication is available from the British Library.
ISBN 0 9505176 1 5

Printed and bound in Great Britain
by Silverscreen, Gateshead

A Celebration of Local Art

By June Sampson

I love Kingston, and have lived in it, worked in it and researched it for nearly 40 years. Even so, I have been astonished to learn just how many public works of art it has. This booklet contains 37 of them. Their dates range from 1707 to 1999, and they vividly reflect changing social tastes, attitudes and values over the past 292 years.

Kingston's earliest known public work of art is the gilded statue of Queen Anne that has stood over the Market Place for nearly three centuries. There was enormous pride and a handsome feast when it was hoisted to its niche in 1707.

Alas, Kingston has been less inclined to celebrate its local art since then. Indeed, its attitude has been so muted that many people assume it has no public works of art at all. How mistaken they are. Our ancient Royal Borough, the oldest in England, has a treasury of public art – but so woefully unlauded that this publication is, I believe, the first ever produced on the subject.

Its 'parents' are the Kingston upon Thames Society and the *Surrey Comet*. The Society supplied the text and most of the photographs, by its past chairman and present committee member Michael Davison, and the design by its vice chairman Tony Leitch, both tireless champions of the Royal Borough. The *Surrey Comet* has provided processing, printing and promotion expertise. Both have helped to finance the project.

Nothing could delight me more. I have been a member of the Kingston Society for close on 30 years, and know what a vital influence for good it is on our local environment and sense of civic pride. And I have been with the *Surrey Comet* since 1973, always proud of the fact that it was born as Kingston's first newspaper in 1854. It promised always to 'promote the good and expose the bad' in local life, and in its 146 years has never missed an issue.

The Kingston Society and the *Comet* are at one with English Heritage in recognising how public art can enrich our everyday lives. English Heritage, marking 2000 as a Year of Public Sculpture, is focusing particularly on statues. Kingston's art portfolio has these, plus many other forms such as stained glass, pictures, mosaics and murals.

In this booklet, Michael Davison takes us on an engrossing tour of them. He starts, appropriately, with our oldest work of art, Queen Anne. Then he leads us on a clockwise circuit of the town centre that encompasses no fewer than 26 art works. Outside the town centre he leads us to 11 more examples of public art to be admired in South and North Kingston, Norbiton, Surbiton and New Malden.

This booklet is at once entertaining and educational. And I guarantee that anyone who follows its mapped tour will, no matter how well they think they know Kingston, see fascinating things they never noticed before.

WHERE TO FIND KINGSTON'S PUBLIC ART

Entries in the town centre are arranged clockwise, starting in the Market Place and finishing at the Guildhall. Entries outside the central area are listed below the map.

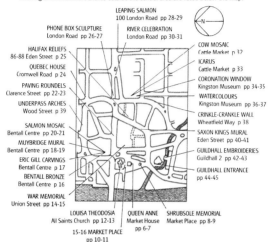

LEAPING SALMON
100 London Road pp 28-29

PHONE BOX SCULPTURE
London Road pp 26-27

RIVER CELEBRATION
London Road pp 30-31

COW MOSAIC
Cattle Market p 32

HALIFAX RELIEFS
86-88 Eden Street p 25

ICARUS
Cattle Market p 33

QUEBEC HOUSE
Cromwell Road p 24

CORONATION WINDOW
Kingston Museum pp 34-35

PAVING ROUNDELS
Clarence Street pp 22-23

WATERCOLOURS
Kingston Museum pp 36-37

UNDERPASS ARCHES
Wood Street p 39

CRINKLE-CRANKLE WALL
Wheatfield Way p 38

SALMON MOSAIC
Bentall Centre pp 20-21

SAXON KINGS MURAL
Eden Street pp 40-41

MUYBRIDGE MURAL
Bentall Centre pp 18-19

GUILDHALL EMBROIDERIES
Guildhall 2 pp 42-43

ERIC GILL CARVINGS
Bentall Centre p 17

GUILDHALL ENTRANCE
pp 44-45

BENTALL BRONZE
Bentall Centre p 16

WAR MEMORIAL
Union Street pp 14-15

LOUISA THEODOSIA
All Saints Church pp 12-13

QUEEN ANNE
Market House
pp 6-7

SHRUBSOLE MEMORIAL
Market Place pp 8-9

15-16 MARKET PLACE
pp 10-11

PUBLIC ART OUTSIDE THE TOWN CENTRE

South Kingston
THUMBPRINT Stanley Picker Gallery, Knights Park :
pp 46-47
WAR MEMORIAL WINDOW County Hall, Penrhyn
Road : pp 48-49
CLOCK TOWER County Hall : back cover
Surbiton
TWO DOLPHINS Maple Road : pp 50-51
CLOCK TOWER Claremont Road : pp 52-53
TRANSPORT MURAL Victoria Road : pp 54-55

Norbiton
FALLOW BUCK 15 Coombe Road : pp 56-57
BURTON MEMORIAL Kingston Cemetery : pp 58-59
New Malden
ARTS & SCIENCES PLAQUES Public Library,
50 Kingston Road : p 60
FAMILY GROUP 53 High Street, New Malden : p 61
North Kingston
BIG SMILING HEAD Kingston College School of Art,
Richmond Road : pp 62-63

Queen Anne
Market House

The statue of Queen Anne that surveys Kingston's Market Place from the balcony of the Market House was made in 1707 to honour the reigning monarch at the time the building was enlarged. Dating from the 16th century, the building was by Anne's time too small for its role as combined Guildhall and law court for the expanding town. The chosen sculptor was Francis Bird, who also created the statue of Queen Anne which gazes down Ludgate Hill from a plinth outside St Paul's Cathedral.

Bird's fee was £47 18s 6d, which the borough treasurer had to advance out of his own pocket as the town was short of money after improving the Guildhall. The raising of the statue into position was celebrated at a grand 'rearing dinner' at the Bull Inn in Thames Street. As the figure was originally designed to stand in a niche, it had no back. In 1840 the Guildhall was entirely rebuilt in its present Italian style, and the statue was given a cement back so that it could stand on a ledge.

In 1994 the statue, which weighs more than a ton, was taken down for major restoration work. It was given a new back made of lead, and layers of paint were stripped off to reveal the fine details of face and costume, which were then embellished with gold leaf. Meanwhile the Market House itself was being grandly restored. By March 1995, when the Mayor reopened the building, Queen Anne was back on her ledge. Being sculpted during the Queen's lifetime, Bird's statue is assumed to be a good likeness. She bears the orb and sceptre, symbols of monarchy, and on her breast is the Order of St George.

Shrubsole Memorial
Market Place

The graceful statue of a woman, balancing a pitcher on her shoulder and holding a child by the hand, commemorates a former Mayor of Kingston who died in January 1880 while handing out packets of tea to 500 poor people at a dinner in Kingston Drill Hall. Henry Shrubsole, a banker who served as mayor for three consecutive years, was so renowned for his good deeds that it was felt his monument should be useful as well as ornamental. At a time when domestic piped water was a luxury, a drinking fountain was the popular choice, and the sum of £500 was raised by public subscription to pay for it.

More than 30 designs were submitted – the drawings for some of them are in Kingston Museum. The chosen sculptor was Francis Williamson, who had his studio in Esher High Street. The 8ft figure, in Sicilian marble, stands on a granite plinth which bears a medallion portrait of Shrubsole on the west side and an inscription praising his work for Kingston on the opposite side. The date of his death is given as January 18, 1880, though in fact he died three days earlier.

Unveiled in 1882 by the Duke of Cambridge, the statue suffered from neglect over the years but was restored in 1995 by NatWest Bank – eventual successors to the bank run by Shrubsole himself – whose premises are only a few yards from the memorial. However, the water that once flowed into the drinking basin no longer runs, and the child stoops among the delicately carved ferns in vain.

15-16 Market Place

The half-timbered Tudor-style frontage dominating the north end of the Market Place, with its royal statues, stained glass and coats of arms, resulted from an unusual collaboration between Dr William Finny, seven times Mayor of Kingston and a keen antiquarian, and Boots the chemists.

In 1909 Boots bought a 19th-century building in the Market Place for a new branch. Knowing that Sir Jesse Boot liked his shops to have an antique look, Finny sketched a design – on a piece of blotting paper, it is said – and sent it to Boot, who ordered his craftsmen to follow it precisely. In 1929 Boots extended the premises and the four statues made by Gilbert Seale in 1909 were increased to six. They include Saxon kings Edward the Elder and Athelstan, King John, who in 1200 gave Kingston its earliest surviving charter, and Elizabeth I who endowed what is now Kingston Grammar School.

Louisa Theodosia
All Saints' Church

The large marble monument that faces the visitor entering Kingston's Parish Church is by one of Britain's most renowned sculptors, Sir Francis Chantrey. Its subject is Louisa Theodosia, first wife of the 2nd Earl of Liverpool, Prime Minister of Britain for 15 years from 1812 to 1827. Their home was at Coombe House, which stood in the Warren Rise area of New Malden before being demolished in 1933. Lord Liverpool owned extensive farmlands in North Kingston, remembered in the name of Liverpool Road. It was Lord Liverpool who in 1825 laid the first stone of Kingston's new bridge, which was opened in 1828 by the Duchess of Clarence, later Queen Adelaide.

Louisa, who died in 1821, was admired for her acts of philanthropy in Kingston: as her monument records, 'she visited the fatherless and widows in their affliction and kept herself unspotted from the world'. Chantrey's figure of Louisa is recognised as one of the finest examples of his art. It was exhibited at the Royal Academy in 1824 and stood for some time in the entrance hall of Coombe House before being placed in All Saints' Church. In 1981 it was the centrepiece of an exhibition at the National Portrait Gallery in London to mark the bicentenary of Chantrey's birth.

A contemporary of Chantrey, John Flaxman, was another of Britain's outstanding sculptors, noted also for his Wedgwood pottery designs. All Saints' Church is fortunate in possessing an example of Flaxman's work, too, in the form of a monumental tablet to Philip Medows over the old north door.

War Memorial
Union Street

When Kingston Council decided to commission a memorial to commemorate the 636 men of Kingston who died in the First World War it ruled out 'effigies of soldiers or engines of war' because these created 'the attitude of mind that makes war possible'. The alternative, provided by the sculptor Richard Goulden, was a group comprising a male figure, striding forward torch in hand, with a child at his side. The tall figure is said to represent the spirit of youth holding aloft a flaming torch as a symbol of self-sacrifice and helping the little ones to avoid the snares and evils encountered on the path through life. Good triumphs over evil, as a serpent is impaled on a drawn sword and a snake lies entangled in bushes.

The sculpture – in bronze, on a granite plinth – was unveiled by Mr F G Penney, MP for Kingston, during an Armistice Day ceremony in 1923. Over the next three years the memorial was given a suitable setting by creating a public garden out of what had once been an overflow burial ground for the Parish Church. The headstones still surrounding the garden are a reminder of its former role, while at one side the original mortuary building survives under a mock-Tudor exterior added in the 1950s.

After the Second World War the wording on the memorial was carefully adapted. With the addition of a single letter it now honoured those who gave their lives in 'The Great Wars', and the dates 1939-1945 were added below. The memorial remains the focus of Kingston's annual Remembrance Day service.

SUN AND IT'S THE MORNING

IN HONOUR OF
THE MEN OF THIS
TOWN WHO GAVE
THEIR LIVES IN
THE GREAT WARS
1914 1919
1939 1945

Leonard Bentall
The Bentall Centre

The life-size bronze statue that looks down from the first floor of the Bentall Centre depicts Leonard Hugh Bentall, who for 33 years guided the fortunes of Bentalls department store. The statue is by Sir William Reid Dick, whose signature appears on its base. It was unveiled in 1944, two years after Bentall's death, and became a familiar landmark above the entrance until the start of the 1990s rebuilding.

In 1909 Bentall inherited a drapery business founded by his father Frank Bentall in 1867, and expanded it into the emporium for which he secured the telephone number 'Kingston 1'. In 1931 he opened his grand new store, to be completed in 1935 with its 700ft curving frontage by Maurice Webb.

By his innovative marketing techniques Bentall made a major contribution to establishing Kingston as a premier shopping centre. He also earned respect by his support for a wide range of borough activities. In 1945 the Mayor of the day called Bentall 'the man who made Kingston'.

Carvings by Eric Gill
The Bentall Centre

To embellish the long facade of his new store, Leonard Bentall commissioned Eric Gill, the renowned sculptor, engraver and typographer of the 1930s. For two upper windows Gill carved borders depicting male and female figures intertwined with foliage whose sinuous shape he used as a symbol of grace and beauty. Gill's drawings for the windows were exhibited at the Royal Academy in 1936. Gill also designed lettering for the building, which was handcarved in his studio by apprentices; this was lost in the 1990s rebuilding but reproduced following the original designs. For the entrances Gill designed panels with the initials of Leonard Bentall and his two sons; a fourth added in 1992 bears the initials of chairman L Edward Bentall.

Eadweard Muybridge Mural
The Bentall Centre

An elephant paces in measured stride, a bird soars aloft and an athlete is caught in mid-sprint, in a mural based on the work of Eadweard Muybridge, the photographer who pioneered moving pictures and is one of Kingston's most renowned sons. Born in High Street in 1830, Muybridge did much of his work in America. In the 1870s he invented the zoopraxiscope, a device that projected a series of images – like those in the mural – in quick succession to give the impression of movement, a major step towards cinematography. In 1894 Muybridge returned to Kingston and died ten years later at 2 Liverpool Road, where there is a plaque. His will said his original zoopraxiscope should never leave Kingston, and it is on show in the Museum. The mural, beside the second-floor crèche, was painted by Jane Gifford with Karen Gregory and Andrew Bradford.

Salmon Mosaic
The Bentall Centre

The three salmon of Kingston's traditional emblem appear to leap in delight at their starring role in the mosaic on the ground floor of the Bentall Centre. The mosaic was designed by Richard Allen of Building Design Partnership, architects for the building, and the motif is repeated in a smaller form in more than 50 three-dimensional plaster roundels set into the supporting columns along the galleries at each level.

The floor mosaic, 6 metres in diameter, is made of granite of different colours from quarries in Sicily and Spain which was cut, shaped, polished and assembled in Italy to Richard Allen's design by craftsmen at Forte del Marmi, near the famous Carrara marble quarries. The wording is spelt out in stainless steel, which is also used in the crown.

From Italy the mosaic was shipped to England in sections, and reassembled on the site. So high were the craftsmen's standards that they insisted on recutting a tiny section of the crown after they inspected the work in the Bentall Centre just before its opening in November 1992: the rejected fragment still resides in Richard Allen's office. The mosaic is walked over daily by thousands of shoppers, but it is in no danger of wearing out: the granite is 20mm thick, bonded to a marble backing as deep again.

Roundel: Old Malden
Clarence Street

As the heraldic emblem for Old Malden in the series of roundels added to Clarence Street in 1993, architect Paul Oakley took the arms of the former borough of Malden and Coombe. The cross refers to Malden's ancient name Maeldune, 'the Hill of the Cross', while the chevrons are from the arms of Merton College, Oxford, founded by Walter de Merton, a Malden landowner.

On July 26, 1989, vehicles drove down Clarence Street for the last time, and pedestrians could wander in safety across what had long been one of Kingston's busiest traffic highways, at last bypassed by the new relief road. Temporary surfacing was replaced in 1993 by the present patterned brickwork, with emblems representing different parts of the Royal Borough.

Roundel: New Malden
Clarence Street

The symbol chosen to represent New Malden on the Clarence
Street paving is the beehive once used on the seal of the
New Malden Local Board. It was intended as a tribute to the
industry applied by the board, which was established in 1866 to
administer New Malden as a separate authority from Kingston.

Other roundels, the pieces for which were cut on site by
craftsman Arthur Mann under the gaze of admiring passers-by,
include the winged lion of St Mark for Surbiton, recalling
St Mark's Church, a stylised St Mary's Church for Chessington,
and for Coombe a wavy pattern representing the water once
piped from springs on Coombe Hill to Hampton Court. A final
roundel for Tolworth, with a striped shop blind to symbolise its
busy Broadway, is to be added in Church Street.

Quebec House
Cromwell Road

Because of its position high above the busy road junction at Kingston Station, it is easy to miss the abstract sculpture on the wall of Quebec House. Made in stainless steel and glass fibre, it was designed as a foil to the geometric lines of the 1960 building, and its colours mirror the window frames. The figure is believed to be by Bianca Treuberg (1913-84), a Munich-born sculptor better known for her portrait busts. Quebec House was named after the battle of 1759 in which British forces ended French power in Canada. It was developed by the Murrayfield Group whose chairman, Field Marshal Sir Claude Auchinleck, named many of its buildings after British military victories.

Halifax Reliefs
86-88 Eden Street

The bearded face that since 1935 has gazed down upon shoppers from above the door of the Halifax Building Society is supposed to be the 'Holy Face' from which the town of Halifax takes its name. According to legend, the village from which Halifax grew was founded on the spot where the face of Christ appeared to shepherds on the surface of a stream. The face was later incorporated in the borough's coat of arms, together with the chequerboard device of the noble appointed to administer affairs in the diocese of Ripon, to which Halifax belonged. The lamb and flag, a Christian symbol, particularly suited an area whose prosperity stemmed from wool and cloth.

Out of Order
London Road

They were the target of as much criticism as acclaim when they were unveiled in 1989 – the mayor of the day later admitted that he had misgivings about performing the ceremony. Yet over the years the 'tumbling telephone boxes' – as they are often called in preference to the name the sculptor gave them – have won admiration and even affection among people in Kingston, and the colourful, eye-catching ensemble is now accepted as almost on a par with the Market Place as a trademark of the town.

'Out of Order' is the brain child of internationally renowned sculptor David Mach, from whom it was commissioned to enhance Kingston's new relief road. By the time Mach was approached he had already conceived the idea of a humorous slant on telephone boxes for a suitable town centre site. The red telephone box, says Mach, is such a typically British feature. 'It is something people have grown up with, part of their cultural history, like the red London bus; when the boxes were under threat, people made it clear they wanted to keep them.'

The opportunity presented by the closure of London Road to through traffic presented Mach with just the site he had envisaged. Having secured 12 cast-off boxes from British Telecom, Mach had to reinforce them with steel frames, after which they were bolted to a concrete base. The Kingston upon Thames Society has done its bit for Mach's telephone boxes: in 1995 members turned out in force on a Sunday morning in May to slap on new paint in the approved shade of red.

Leaping Salmon
100 London Road

Three salmon have been an emblem of Kingston for more than 500 years. They were therefore a natural choice of subject for the sculpture commissioned from David Wynne by John Hickman of Kingstons Estate Developers as the centrepiece of a fountain to stand outside a new London Road office building. It was unveiled in June 1980 by Lord Home of Hirsel – the former Sir Alec Douglas-Home, Prime Minister from 1963 to 1964. The stainless-steel salmon, mouths agape, still cavort cheerfully among the shrubs on their brick-walled island, though the fountain no longer plays.

The three salmon fisheries in the Thames which contributed to Kingston's medieval prosperity were first referred to in William I's Domesday Book, the national survey commissioned by the king in 1085 and carried out during the following year. As a plaque below the sculpture records, the salmon first appeared in 1441 on a seal granted to 'the baylifs and fremen of the Towne of Kingstone uppon Thames' by a charter of Henry VI. In 1572 they became part of the original coat of arms of the Royal Borough.

David Wynne, whose connection with the area dates from his long residence in Wimbledon, has contributed two other sculptures to Kingston's townscape – 'Two Dolphins' in Maple Road and the 'Fallow Buck' in Coombe Road.

River Celebration
London Road

Roadside sculpture was an integral part of Kingston Council's plan for the new relief road built in the 1980s. For the promontory at the corner of London Road and Fairfield North it commissioned Carole Hodgson, who had already made the 'Icarus' bronze for the Cattle Market car park stairwell, to design a new bronze sculpture celebrating Kingston's association with the River Thames.

Hodgson's response was to create a standing figure which seems to revolve like a pirouetting dancer, suggesting the way the river twists and turns. The figure is represented standing among sections of Kingston Bridge and parts of boats, and when it rains the water cascading down its many surfaces gives the impression of a fountain. The sculpture, unveiled in 1990, is elevated on a tall eight-sided plinth, echoing the turret of Lovekyn Chapel which stands opposite – a tribute from one of Kingston's newest pieces of sculpture to one of its most ancient buildings, dating from nearly 700 years earlier.

Advising Kingston Council on sculpture for the relief road Ainslie Yule, Reader in Sculpture at Kingston University, arranged competitions for key sites, and invited chosen artists and sculptors to present ideas. Council officers, aided by expert assessors, made the final selection, which as well as 'River Celebration' included the telephone-box sculpture in London Road, the 'crinkle-crankle' wall on Wheatfield Way, the mosaic in the Apple Market car park, and the arch-like motifs on the wall of the underpass near Kingston Station.

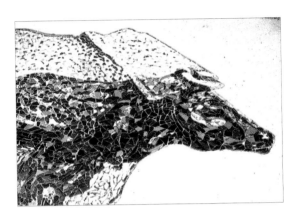

Cow Mosaic
Cattle Market

The cattle market that was held on the site regularly until the Second World War gave sculptor David Mach a natural choice of subject for his mosaic in the stairwell of the car park opened in 1987. Mach explains that he devised the multi-coloured mosaic cow to bring brightness to a dark area. Its features have a blocked-in background, like a child's wooden farmyard figure, giving it a three-dimensional effect that seems to raise it from the floor. The tiny fragments used to make up the mosaic are not special artist's materials but cut from household tiles of the sort anyone can buy in a DIY store. Mach likes to make his sculptures from familiar, everyday materials, to introduce people to them through a medium they can easily recognise.

Icarus
Cattle Market

The airborne group in the Cattle Market stairwell marks a 75-year association between Kingston and the aviation industry. It began in 1912 when Tom Sopwith set up a factory in Canbury Park Road; the sculpture shows the Sopwith Camel in the hands of Icarus, the legendary Greek figure whose wings were held in place by wax which melted when he flew too close to the sun. The complete group includes a spaceman holding a Harrier, salmon leaping over Kingston Bridge and, below, two other made-in-Kingston aircraft, the Hawk and the Hurricane. The bronze is by Carole Hodgson, who at the time of the British Aerospace commission in 1986 was a tutor in Kingston Polytechnic's Canbury Park Road site, birthplace of the Camel.

Coronation Window
Kingston Museum, Wheatfield Way

Two coronations separated by 1000 years of English history are linked in one of six stained-glass windows in Kingston Museum. Edward, also called Eadweard, the Elder was crowned in 900 – at Kingston, the window confidently asserts, though historians say this cannot be proved. A window designed to celebrate the thousandth anniversary of this event was unveiled in 1902 just before the coronation of Edward VII, and the design incorporates his coat of arms as well as arms representing seven Saxon kings associated with Kingston.

The six windows, commemorating aspects of Kingston's history, were designed by Dr William Finny, seven times Mayor of Kingston and a keen local historian, for Kingston's old Town Hall, now the Market House. They were moved to the Museum in 1936 when the Council built the new Guildhall.

In 1927, citing references to Kingston as a royal town in Saxon times, Dr Finny successfully petitioned George V to confirm Kingston's status as one of only four boroughs in England and Wales to be called Royal, and another of the windows he presented commemorates this accolade. Other windows commemorate the thousandth anniversary of the accession of King Athelstan, and the 700th anniversary of the granting of Kingston's first Charter by King John in 1200. Panes of glass from an earlier Tudor Guildhall are framed in a fifth window, while the sixth shows characters such as the Fool, the May Queen and the Minstrel who appeared in plays and dances performed in Kingston in Tudor times.

'Military Parade'
Kingston Museum

This painting of a parade in Kingston Market Place is the only surviving illustration of the uniforms worn by the Surrey Militia, raised in 1798 against the threat of Napoleonic invasion, with its headquarters in Kingston. On the left is the Tudor Guildhall, with its open trading area, which was demolished in 1838. The picture was drawn in pencil, ink and watercolour around 1805 by John Nixon, who made many sketching tours in Southern England. Nixon's contemporary Thomas Rowlandson also drew several scenes in Kingston, and nine of these are in Kingston Museum. One of Kingston's most treasured paintings is a 1706 portrait of Queen Anne by Sir Godfrey Kneller, which hangs in the Guildhall and can be seen by prior arrangement.

'Kingston Bridge'
Kingston Museum

An impression of Kingston Bridge in pen and watercolour made in 1955 shows the timber-yard which once stood at the foot of the bridge on the Kingston bank. The artist, Frank Archer, was Head of Fine Art at Kingston School of Art, which is now part of Kingston University. This is one of a number of paintings that Archer has contributed to Kingston Museum's Brill Collection, a series of commissioned topographical paintings that record the changing face of the borough. The collection is named after Reginald Brill, Head of Kingston School of Art. It lapsed in 1971, but was revived in 1997 on the initiative of the Friends of Kingston Museum and Heritage Service, and now holds more than 70 paintings, which are on show in rotation.

Crinkle-crankle wall
Wheatfield Way

At more than 500 ft long, the undulating wall on the east side of Wheatfield Way is probably Britain's longest public sculpture. It is a sculpture with a function, designed to form both an attractive boundary and also a 'sound barrier' between the road and the houses behind it. Like other relief road sculpture, its designer was chosen by competition. The first 300ft of artist Nigel Hall's crinkle-crankle wall, named after its snake-like shape which is more familiar in East Anglia than in Surrey, received a 1991 Kingston upon Thames Society Townscape Award. It was later extended to its full length, and contains 50,500 bricks, many hand-made to follow the curves.

Underpass Arches
Wood Street

The decorative brickwork in the underpass beside Kingston Station was designed by Colin Nicholas, a lecturer in sculpture at the former Kingston Polytechnic. Invited to enhance this section of the relief road, Nicholas broke up the monotony of the large areas of brick in the complex of roads and walkways by a series of arches in brick of contrasting colours. The main arches are in blue brick, hand-made to protrude from the wall, and within them are secondary arches in yellow, charcoal and red – 'executed with great skill', said the Kingston upon Thames Society in giving the arches a 1990 Townscape Award, 'and following the curve of the wall with deceptive ease'.

Saxon Kings Mural
Eden Street

The seven Saxon kings who may have been crowned on the Coronation Stone in Kingston during the 10th century are the main subjects of the mural designed and modelled in 67 pieces of stoneware clay by Maggie Humphrey, an artist from North Wales. The brilliant colours catch the sunshine as brightly today as when the mural was unveiled by the Mayor in 1985.

Eadred, crowned in 946, was ill for most of his life, so his mother who ruled for him appears above his portrait. Below the kings runs the River Thames, with boats, a ducking stool for punishing scolds – mentioned in 16th-century accounts of Kingston – and the familiar salmon. At the foot of the mural a frieze depicts buildings and characters of Eden Street in the 19th century – butcher, baker, cobbler, midwife, fiddler – as recalled in a book by George Ayliffe, who sits in the centre.

The Kingston Embroideries
Guildhall 2

Needle and thread rather than paintbox and brush were used to create the four panels illustrating landmarks of the Royal Borough that hang along the first-floor balcony of the entrance hall of Guildhall 2. Two panels are devoted to the town centre, and in them the keen eye can pick out more than 30 separate scenes, from ancient almshouses to modern pubs, from market traders' stalls to the chimneys of the Power Station demolished in 1994. A third panel features Chessington, Tolworth and Surbiton, and the fourth depicts scenes in Malden, Coombe and Norbiton. The panels are linked by a stylised Thames flowing along their bases.

The embroideries, each 6ft long and 3ft wide, represent two years' painstaking work by no fewer than 53 members of the Kingston and District branch of the Embroiderers' Guild, to the design of Margaret Rivers. The chairman of the branch, Margaret Humphrey, who directed the operation, photographed a wide selection of houses, churches, monuments and offices. She asked each volunteer needlewoman to choose a scene, then go out and study it carefully before plying her needle. The stitchwork of the buildings was done in crewel wool on canvas, while trees and gardens were worked in machine embroidery and then applied. The lettering is in padded leather.

Begun in April 1987, the completed panels were presented to the borough in May 1989, and the Mayor, Councillor the Rev Michael Mannall, unveiled a plaque to commemorate their hanging in the Guildhall.

43

The Guildhall Entrance

Horses prance above the wave crests to symbolise Kingston's waterside location in carvings at the entrance to the Guildhall, opened in 1935. Between them, realistically silver against more symbolic waves, are the three salmon of the borough emblem, while classical figures hold an anchor and a horn of plenty. The sculptors were Walter and Donald Gilbert. The Guildhall, built in Portland stone on the site of municipal offices in the 18th-century Clattern House, replaced the old Town Hall – now the Market House – as the borough's administrative centre. Only 12 months separate the date on the foundation stone from that of the opening ceremony. The architect, Maurice Webb, also designed the Bentalls store completed in the same year.

Dusting the Giant
Stanley Picker Gallery, Knights Park

The giant bronze thumbprint commissioned for the opening of Kingston University's Stanley Picker Gallery in 1997 has become a familiar sight to walkers using the path that passes the Gallery and crosses the Hogsmill by a little footbridge. Its sculptor, Brian McCann, held a Picker Fellowship at Kingston University in 1983-4, and still lectures there.

McCann explains that the sculpture's title refers to the way in which archaeologists dust the surface of their 'finds' when bringing to light and protecting the giant achievements of past cultures. Hands are 'the instruments by which we make things happen'. The thumbprint echoes natural features of the setting: 'people may see it as a tree . . . a spider's web between the shrubs . . . or even a reflection of the tumbling Hogsmill.'

After winning a competition for the sculpture, McCann tested three versions in wood on the site to get the scale right. Then he made a skeleton thumbprint in wood in six sections – using his own thumb as model – and moulded paper pulp round it. A foundry cased each section in plaster, then poured bronze into the moulds; the bronze burned out the wood and pulp and solidified to fill the space, retaining the rippling effect of the moulding. The sections were then welded together.

The Stanley Picker Gallery is home to changing exhibitions of contemporary art and sculpture. It is named after the late industrialist and art collector who was a major benefactor of the University's School of Fine Art. His former home in Coombe contains his outstanding art collection, open by appointment.

War Memorial Window
County Hall, Penrhyn Road

Afternoon sunlight throws into relief the brilliant blue, turquoise and gold representation in stained glass of St George slaying the Dragon, chosen as the motif for Surrey County Council's war memorial window on the central staircase of County Hall. The inscription commemorates not only the fallen of the Second World War, but also the 'courage and fortitude of the people of Surrey'. The window was commissioned in June 1949 from the ecclesiastical art craftsmen G Maile and Son, for £1,500. The approved design, it was recorded in the Council's minutes, 'has been designed to give a radiating effect, and the whole effect of the window will be pleasing and distinctive'.

The new home for Surrey County Council was built in 1893, after fierce rivalry from other contenders anxious for the status of county town. It was designed to impress late 19th-century Kingston, and it remains one of the town's most imposing buildings. Designed by Charles Henry Howell, the architect also of London's County Hall, it was built in Portland stone that glistens like marble in the sunlight. The building's most striking feature is its tall clock tower, topped by a belltower with an elaborate cupola (see back cover). At its corners, sculptures by Farmer and Brindley represent the four seasons. Spring, with a horn of plenty, faces south-east and Summer, bearing flowers, faces south-west; Autumn, with sickle and sheaf, looks to the north-west and Winter, warmly clad, to the north-east. The building faced Grove Road, renamed Penrhyn Road in honour of the County Council's first chairman, E H Leycester-Penrhyn.

Two Dolphins
Sutherland House, Maple Road, Surbiton

Swimming with dolphins off the coasts of Wales, Ireland and North Carolina gave sculptor David Wynne the affection for the friendly sea creatures which have made them one of the favourite subjects of his art. The bronze commissioned by Kingstons Estate Developers and placed in 1988 outside Sutherland House, on the corner of Maple Road and Surbiton Crescent, depicts two dolphins apparently gambolling in space, supported only by their tails on a slender plinth. The leaping and twisting of dolphins at play with which Wynne grew familiar is vividly caught in a group that appears in lively movement from every angle.

Dolphins also figure in two of David Wynne's best known works in Central London: 'Boy with Dolphin' stands on the corner of Cheyne Walk and Beaufort Street at the north end of Albert Bridge, and 'Girl with Dolphin' stands on the Thames embankment just downstream from Tower Bridge.

A sculptor for more than 50 years and enjoying international renown, Wynne designed the 50p coin marking Britain's entry into the European Community in 1973; this featured a ring of nine hands, for which members of his own family provided the models. More recently, Wynne created the controversial Queen Mother's Gates at Hyde Park Corner, unveiled in 1993, their painted bronze displaying a brightly coloured lion and unicorn.

Coronation Clock Tower
Claremont Road, Surbiton

As many as 116 architects competed to design a memorial for Surbiton to commemorate the Coronation of Edward VII in 1902. The winner, John Johnson, designed a Gothic clock tower which, after long delays caused by slow progress in raising funds, was completed in Bath stone in 1908, only two years before the king died. In the absence of any inscription, the only clues indicating the purpose for which the clock tower was built are a bronze medallion of the king in one of the arched niches, and the initials of Edward and his queen, Alexandra, on the wind vane.

In early photographs white stone figures can be seen at each corner of the plinth, but it is believed that one of these collapsed so the remainder were removed. Railings which originally surrounded the clock tower were removed in 1940 to make munitions and not replaced.

In 1963 the clock tower survived calls for it to be demolished to save the expense of restoring it. This time, however, the people of Surbiton were more generous and quickly raised £328 for repairs. Further restoration brought the clock back to working order for the year 2000.

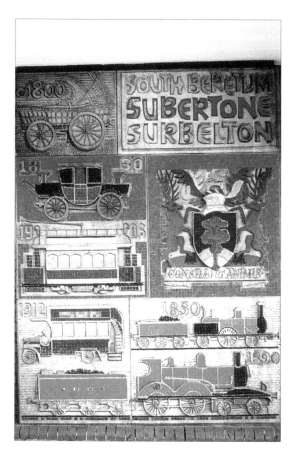

Transport Through The Ages
Victoria Road, Surbiton

The railway which created Surbiton when it arrived in 1838 inspired two ceramic murals on the wall of Sainsbury's. The changing shape of the locomotive over 60 years is shown in profiles made from tiny squares of coloured glass set in concrete. Other forms of transport represented include a stage coach of the 1800s, a trolley bus – familiar in Surbiton until about 1960 – a modern bus and a river steamer. Local buildings are depicted, together with the badge of the London & South-Western Railway and the coat of arms of the former borough of Surbiton. The murals were made in 1980 by Henry Collins and Joyce Pallot, a husband-and-wife team of Colchester artists, after detailed research into Surbiton history.

Fallow Buck
Kingstons House, 15 Coombe Road

When John Hickman opened new offices for Kingstons Estate Developers in Coombe Road, near Norbiton Station, in 1981 he sought a decorative feature for the forecourt and turned to the sculptor David Wynne for a suitable bronze. Wynne's sculpture 'Leaping Salmon' was already a feature of another Kingstons Estates development in London Road. For the Coombe Road building Wynne offered a Fallow Buck, appropriate for a site so near the Kingston Gate into Richmond Park.

David Wynne lived and worked in Wimbledon for 30 years, and used to ride regularly in Richmond Park among its herds of grazing red and fallow deer. The buck he has depicted, apparently startled by a sudden noise as it stands by a rock-girt pool poised ready for flight, has the broad-bladed antlers of a mature male fallow deer in summer, the size and points of its antlers suggesting an age of three years or more.

Martyn Hickman, managing director of the present owners of Kingstons House, says he enjoys watching passing shoppers and Norbiton Station commuters pause to admire the buck in the changing light. Families often linger there, children dabbling their fingers in the pool and listening to the water that in summer splashes down the rock shelves behind the deer.

Burton Memorial
Kingston Cemetery

A tragedy which struck a prominent local family in 1908 led to the raising of a memorial in Kingston Cemetery which today has Grade II listed protection. The figure of a winged girl in greening bronze, with upraised face and arms, stands in memory of Dorothy, 'our darling Dolly', the younger daughter of Arthur and Florence Burton of Thames Ditton, who died on April 28, 1908, in her fifteenth year, 'after a long and painful illness borne with patience and cheerfulness'. The bronze was designed by Richard Goulden, and stands to the left of the drive, 100 yards inside the arched entrance to the cemetery.

The grieving father, Arthur Bryan Burton, had in 1902 become the proprietor of the Statue Foundry in Thames Ditton, and in his hands it became one of the major foundries in Britain. To Burton's workshops on Summer Road leading sculptors brought their models for casting; among them were the figure of 'Physical Energy' by G F Watts, in Kensington Gardens, and the 32ft high figure of 'Peace', with a four-horse chariot, by Adrian Jones, above the arch at Hyde Park Corner.

After the First World War the Burton Foundry produced war memorials – including the one in Kingston, also by Goulden. Burton was admired as a craftsman and a benevolent employer. He became a respected figure in the community: a tablet in the Baptist Church Hall was laid by Burton when the building was extended in 1932. The pedestal supporting the memorial to 'Dolly' also records the death of Burton's wife Florence in 1932, and of Burton himself a year later, at 73.

Arts and Sciences Plaques
Public Library, 50 Kingston Road, New Malden

For the themes of his nine plaques on the walls of New Malden Library, sculptor T Mewburn Crook appropriately chose the divisions of the Dewey System of library classification. Each panel symbolises a separate field of human learning. History is represented by Ancient Egypt, a barque and Stephenson's 'Rocket'. For Literature, Shakespeare is joined by the masks of Comedy and Tragedy. Fine Art embraces a Grecian capital and the tools of architect, painter and sculptor, and Applied Science offers a lighthouse, a steamship and a flying boat. The plaques mask fresh-air inlets to the library, which was completed in 1941 and from the air has the shape of an open book.

Family Group
Tudor Williams, 53 High Street, New Malden

High on the wall, mother, father and three children link hands as if swirling round in a dance. The group, presented by architect Geoffrey Uffindell who enlarged the store in the 1970s, was created by sculptors Derek and Patricia Freeborn, who lived for six years on a houseboat at Kingston Bridge. 'We thought a family group would be an appropriate tribute to a firm that had been a family store in New Malden since 1913,' says Derek. 'We'd been looking at our own children playing in a circle waist-deep in a swimming pool, and this seemed the right perspective for the chosen position, high up against a wall.' The figures are in a glass-fibre compound over a steel framework.

Big Smiling Head

Kingston College School of Art, Richmond Road

One of the latest additions to Kingston's collection of public art is a giant head unveiled as recently as December, 1999, and placed in the forecourt of Kingston College's School of Art and Design to cheer North Kingston commuters heading for their morning trains. 'Everyone understands a beaming smile', say its designers Paul Osborn and Mike Pugh. 'We wanted to make something with a universal message.'

To make 'Big Smiling Head', Osborn and Pugh directed the work of 16 adults with learning difficulties at the Causeway Day Centre, New Malden. The amateur sculptors were taken from New Malden for a few hours every week to work alongside art students at Kingston College, and the great head, 10ft high and weighing 2 tons, gradually evolved over a period of four years. It was created with 3in thick layers of plaster of Paris over a frame of steel and chicken wire, finished off with acrylic paints and coats of lacquer, then set on a concrete plinth.

After examining the effect on 'Big Head' of exposure to the elements during the winter months, the designers withdrew it temporarily from display while remedial work was done to make it more robust and weather-resistant. With its new extra-hard sealant they are confident it will be there to stay, with occasional repainting to preserve its bronze sheen. 'We hope it will become a popular landmark – and a talking point', say the designers. Arthur Cotterell, Principal of Kingston College, hopes that the head will be the first item in a collection of sculptures in the college forecourt.

'BIG SMILING HEAD'
CAUSEWAY CENTRE

WORKS OF ART AND THEIR ARTISTS

MONUMENTS ON RECORD

Kingston's sculptural works are to be included in the National Recording Project – a nation-wide survey of public sculpture organised by the Public Monuments and Sculpture Association. An illustrated catalogue of monuments in South-west London is also in preparation. Research for both projects is being conducted by the History of Art Department of the Faculty of Design, Kingston University.

ILLUSTRATIONS

All photographs are © Michael Davison with the exception of:
pp 31, 33 © Carole Hodgson; pp 35, 36, 37 © Kingston Museum and Heritage Service: Nixon watercolour purchased with assistance from the Beecroft Trust;
pp 29, 38 © Davina Thackara; p 45. © Kingston Embroiderers' Guild.